The Jungle Book

EASY PIANO

Walt Disney's

ISBN 978-0-634-00380-6

Wonderland Music Company, Inc.

DISTRIBUTED BY

HAL•LEONARD®
CORPORATION
7777 W. BLUEMOUND RD. P.O. BOX 13819 MILWAUKEE, WI 53213

Visit Hal Leonard Online at
www.halleonard.com

EASY PIANO

CONTENTS

COLONEL HATHI'S MARCH
(The Elephant Song)

Words and Music by RICHARD M. SHERMAN
and ROBERT B. SHERMAN

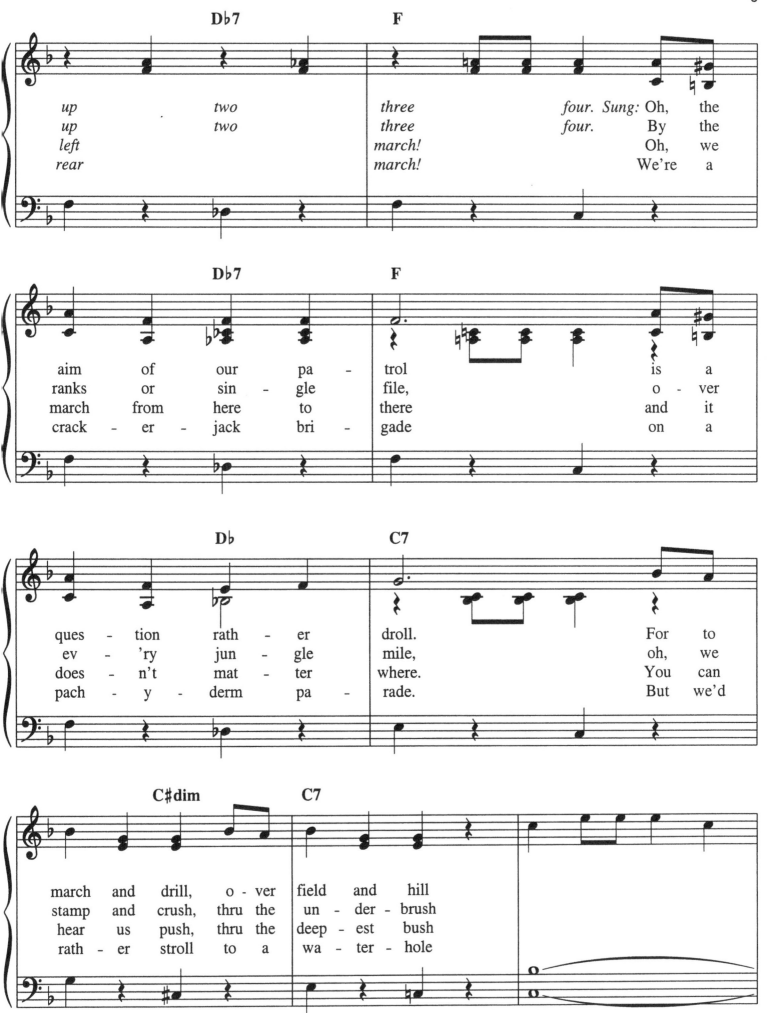

is a mil – i – tar – y goal! Is a
in a mil – i – tar – y style! In a
with a mil – i – tar – y air! With a
for a fur – lough in the shade! For a

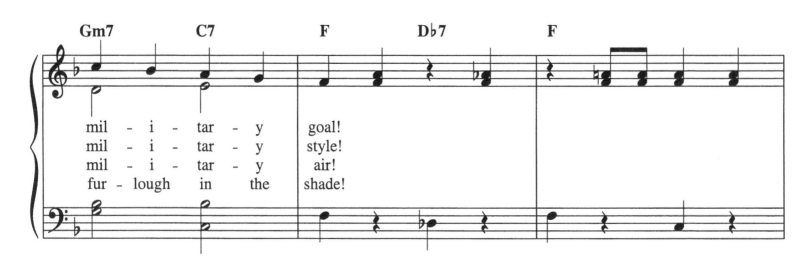

mil – i – tar – y goal!
mil – i – tar – y style!
mil – i – tar – y air!
fur – lough in the shade!

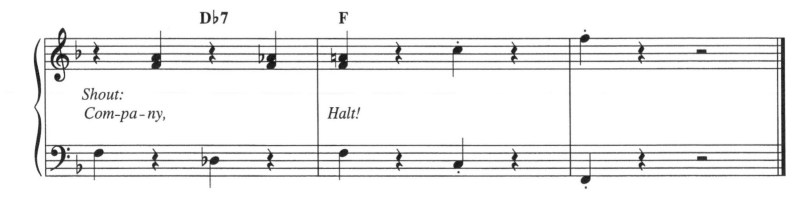

Shout:
Com-pa - ny,   *Halt!*

THE BARE NECESSITIES

Words and Music by
TERRY GILKYSON

8

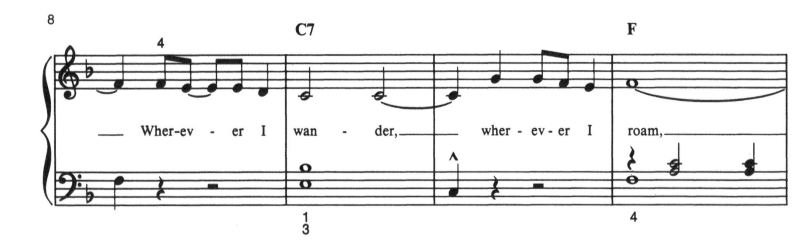

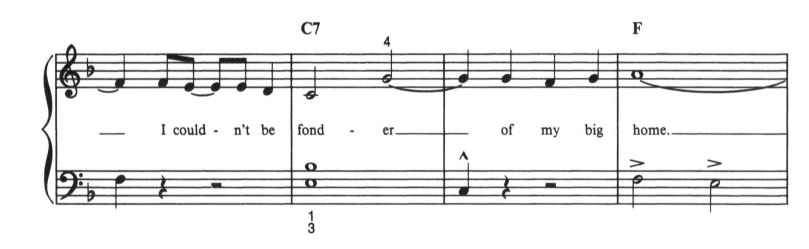

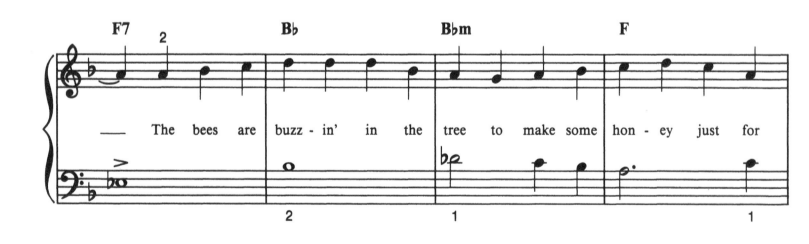

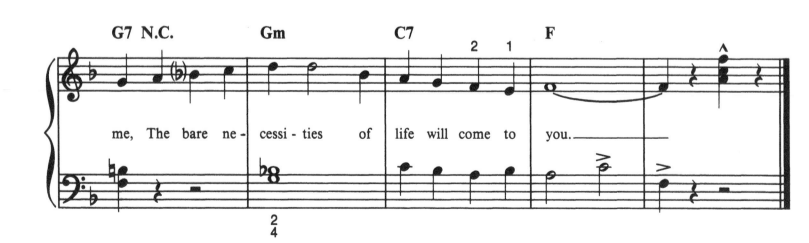

I WAN'NA BE LIKE YOU
(The Monkey Song)

Words and Music by RICHARD M. SHERMAN
and ROBERT B. SHERMAN

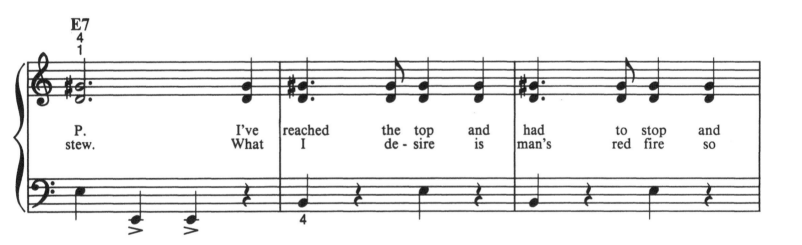

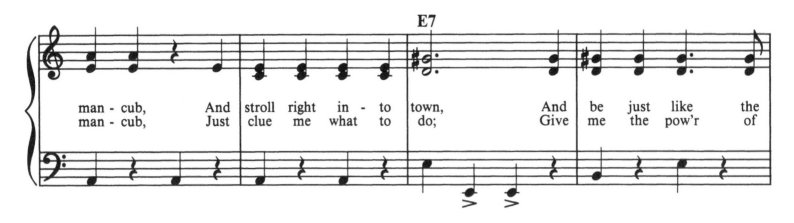

man - cub,　And　stroll right in - to　town,　　And　be　just　like　the
man - cub,　Just　clue　me　what　to　do;　　Give　me　the　pow'r　of

oth - er　men,　I'm　tired　of　mon - key - in'　'round!
man's　red　flow'r　and　make　my　dream＿ come　true!　Oh

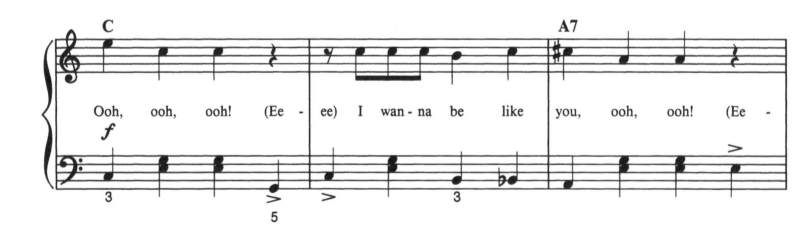

Ooh,　ooh,　ooh!　(Ee - ee)　I　wan - na　be　like　you,　ooh,　ooh!　(Ee -

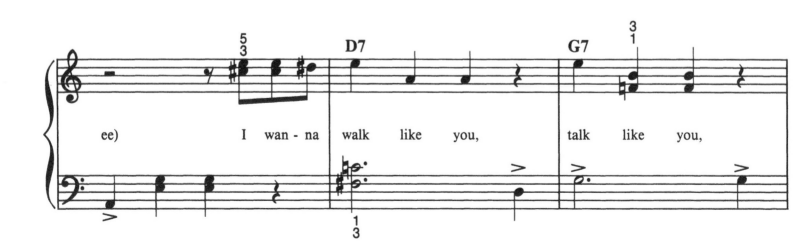

ee)　　I　wan - na　walk　like　you,　　talk　like　you,

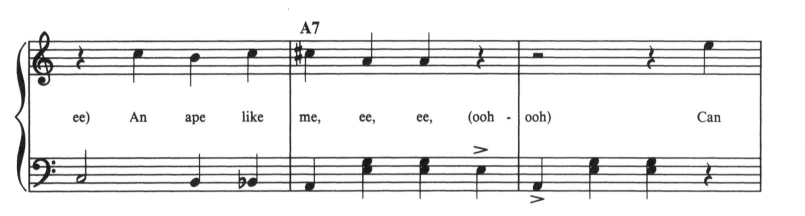

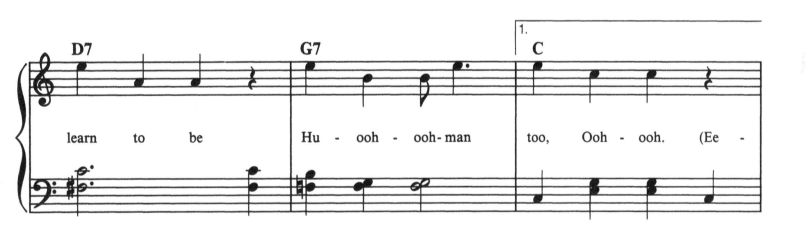

TRUST IN ME
(The Python's Song)

Words and Music by RICHARD M. SHERMAN
and ROBERT B. SHERMAN

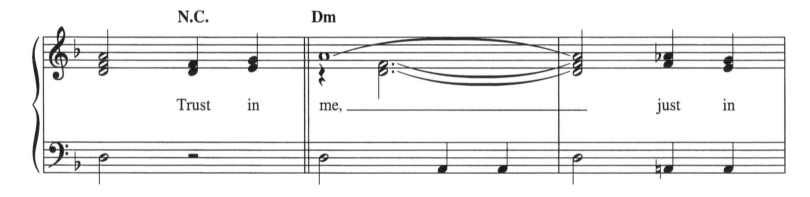

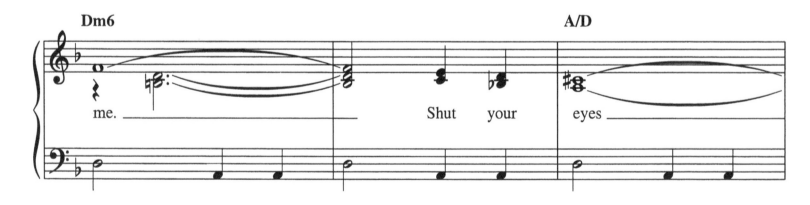

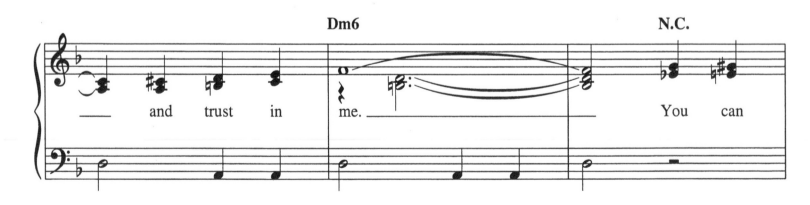

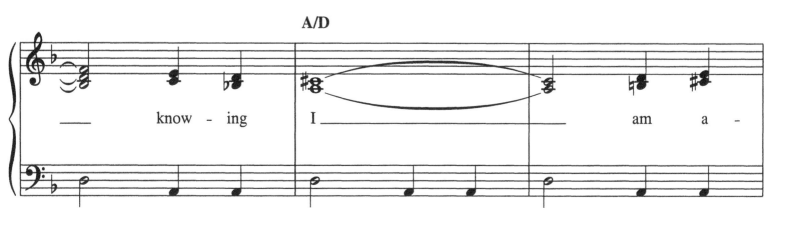

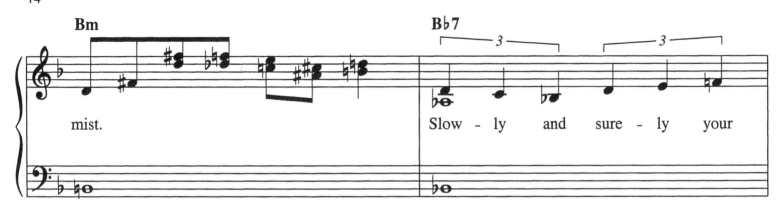

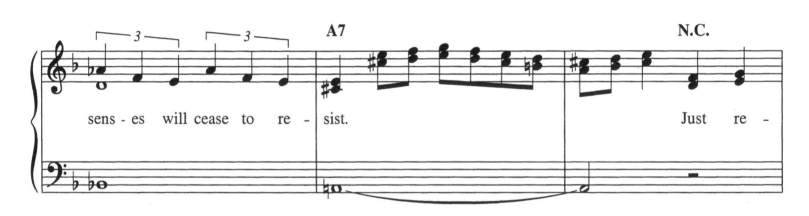

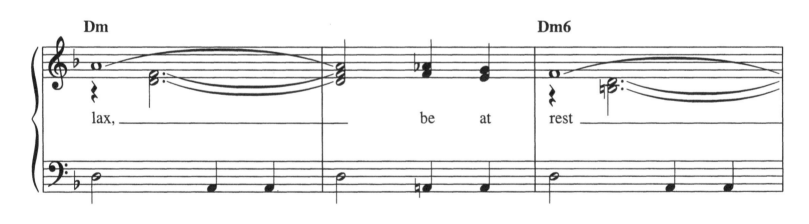

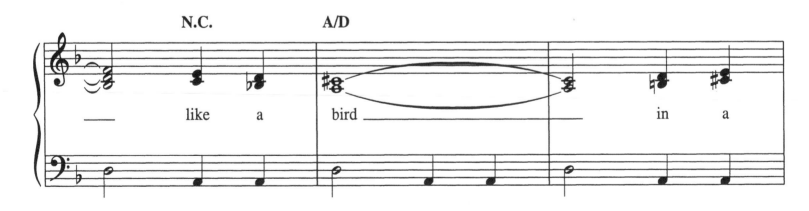

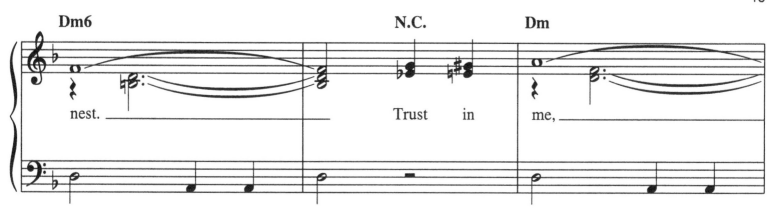

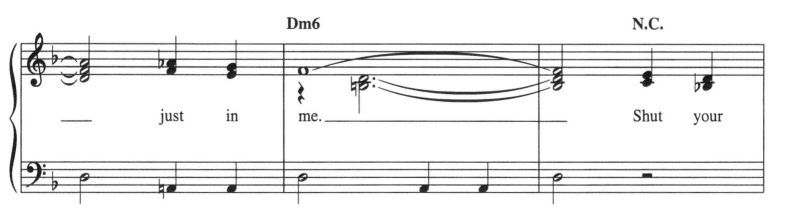

THAT'S WHAT FRIENDS ARE FOR
(The Vulture Song)

Words and Music by RICHARD M. SHERMAN
and ROBERT B. SHERMAN

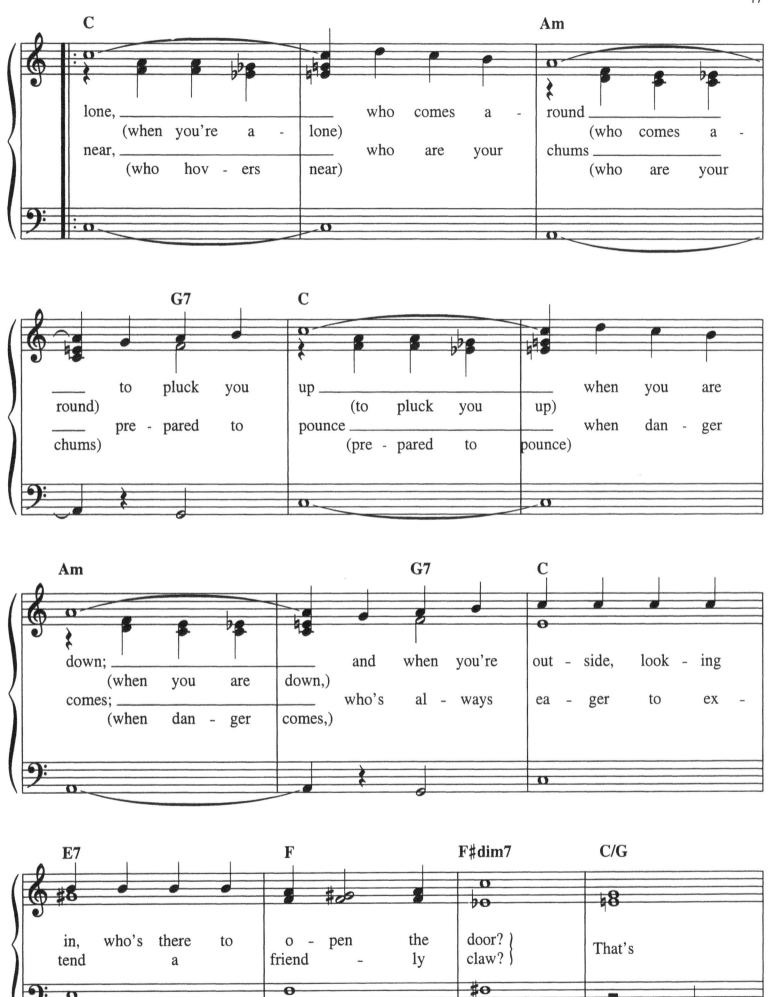

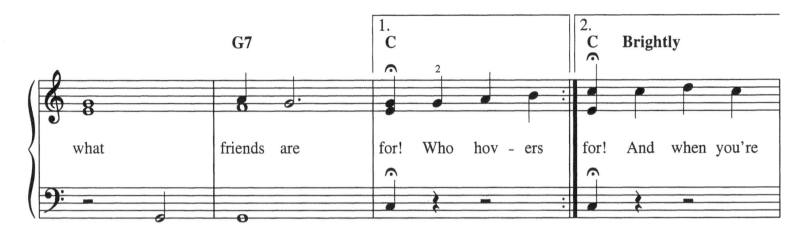

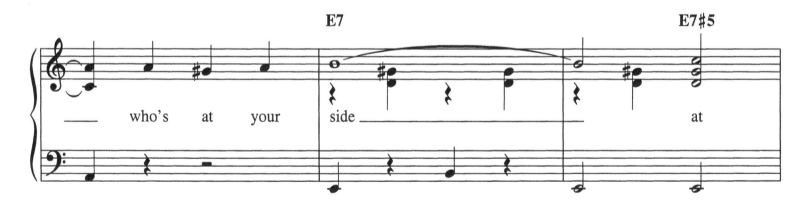

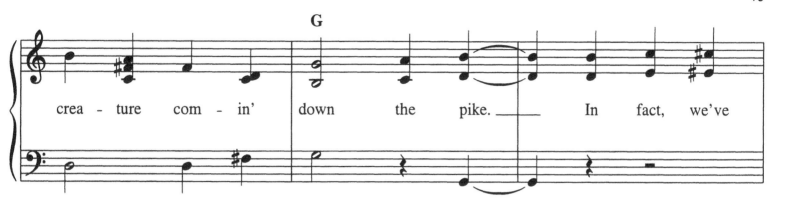

creature com-in' down the pike. ___ In fact, we've

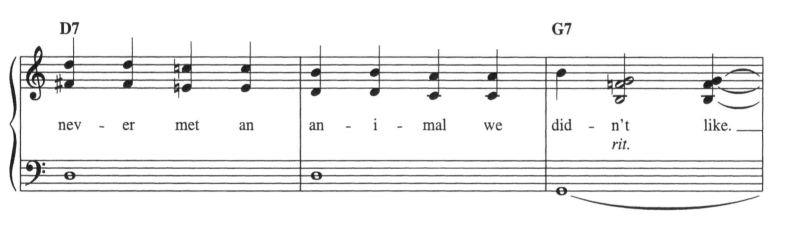

nev-er met an an-i-mal we did-n't like. ___
rit.

Did-n't like. So, you can

see ___ we're friends in need. ___
(So you can see) (we're friends in

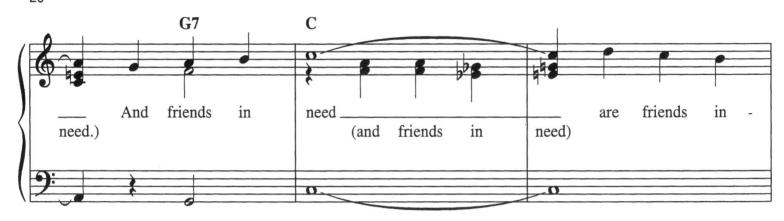

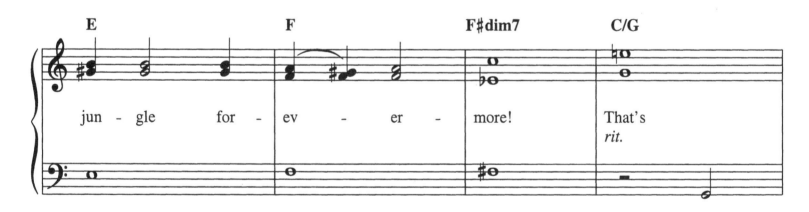

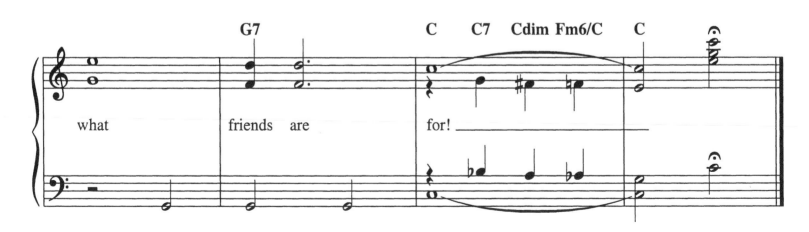

MY OWN HOME
(Jungle Book Theme)

Words and Music by RICHARD M. SHERMAN
and ROBERT B. SHERMAN

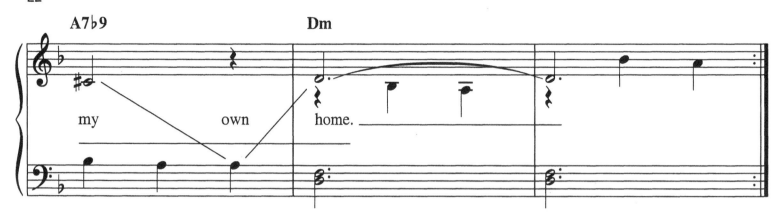

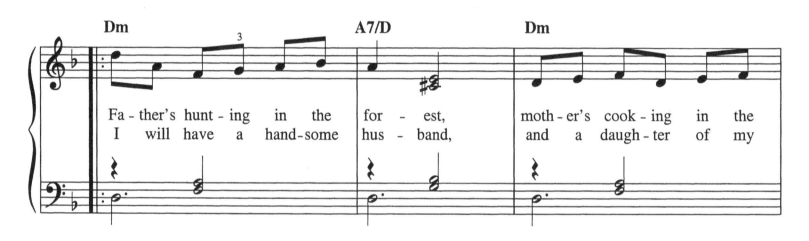

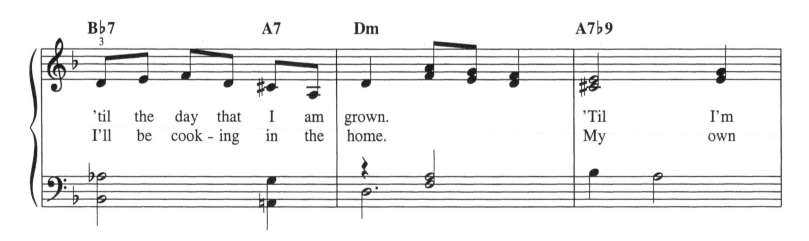